The **Hostess**

Twinkies BRAND

COOKBOOK

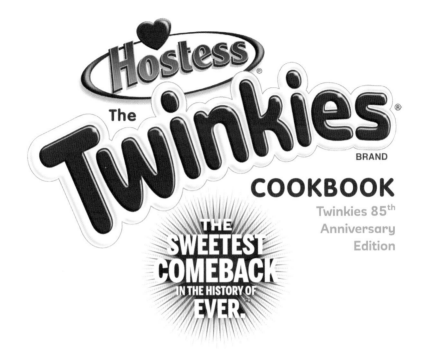

Hostess

The Twinkies® BRAND

COOKBOOK

Twinkies 85th
Anniversary
Edition

THE SWEETEST COMEBACK IN THE HISTORY OF EVER.™

A New Sweet and Savory Recipe Collection
for America's Most Iconic Snack Cake

TEN SPEED PRESS
Berkeley

Library of Congress Cataloging-in-Publication Data
The Twinkies cookbook : a new sweet and savory recipe collection for
America's most iconic snack cake hostess. — Revised edition.
    pages cm
Includes bibliographical references and index.
 1. Cake. 2. Desserts. 3. Twinkies (Trademark)
 TX771.T85 2015
 641.86'53—dc23
                        2014048733

Hardcover ISBN: 978-1-60774-771-0
eBook ISBN: 978-1-60774-772-7

Printed in China

Design by Kara Plikaitis

10 9 8 7 6 5 4 3 2 1

First Revised Edition

twinkie

Acknowledgments

Hostess Brands, LLC, the maker of Hostess® Twinkies®, would like to thank the following individuals and organizations for making this special recipe collection possible:

C. Dean Metropoulos & Co. and Apollo Global Management for helping to ensure a bright future for one of America's greatest brands;

All of the Hostess Brands' employees who devoted their time and talents to this project;

Hannah Arnold, who conceived the original *The Twinkies Cookbook* and this sequel and wrote the introduction chronicling the role of Twinkies in our history and society, and the team at LAK Public Relations;

Kathy Moore and Roxanne Wyss of The Electrified Cooks for expertly testing—and tasting—these recipes;

And especially the legions of loyal Twinkies fans who have made the sweet treat the gold standard and continue to be the cream of the cake!

For several generations, Hostess Twinkies have tantalized America's taste buds with a sweet and irresistible charm, creating a lasting and indelible impression—a magical mystique that seemed certain to live on forever.

Until the unthinkable happened.

At the end of 2012, eighty-two years after the golden cream-filled treat danced onto the snack cake stage, its future was in doubt. The brand's then-owners announced plans to shutter operations and Hostess products began disappearing from store shelves. Long the fodder of urban legends, Twinkies' shelf life was expiring.

As obituary writers shed sugary tears penning the loss of a legacy, a groundswell of public emotion began to ensue. The social media universe erupted with passionate posts, headstonelike hashtags of the distraught. "No more Twinkies, No more Ho Hos, No more reason to live," read one tweet. Grassroots "Save the Twinkie" campaigns sprouted in the heartland. One YouTube video attracted more than five million views. Politico even reported on a "White House petition" asking "President Obama to nationalize the Twinkie industry" to save "the popular junk food from possible extinction."

Consumers simply couldn't imagine a world without Twinkies.

Hollywood heavyweights joined the chorus. "Celebrities Mourn the Demise of the Hostess Twinkie," reported the Huffington Post, featuring screen shots of tweets from actors, including Rob Lowe who said, "Mr. President, the time for intervention is now!"

As word of the Twinkies travesty spread, shoppers began stockpiling treats amid hoarding frenzies, many standing in line for hours to pick up the last of the lot. Some purchased for stocking stuffers and others to freeze in perpetuity. Local restaurants offered special Twinkie-themed promotions as farewell tributes to the familiar friend. And collectors sprung into action as the Associated Press reported Twinkies were "being sold on the Internet like exquisite delicacies," with other outlets noting "Twinkie-pocalypse Fears" and "Twinkiegeddon" as black market prices skyrocketed. One seller reportedly hoped to fetch $5,000 for a Twinkie and the "opportunity to own a piece of history, a delicious piece at that." "Twinkie Madness Grips Chicago," said Fox News, "as the last shipments of Hostess products hit shelves."

The message was clear: consumers were not going to let the beloved Twinkie twinkle off into the sunset. From the surreal to the sublime, it was a snacktravaganza for the ages.

By the end of the year, Twinkies were no longer in stores. But a miracle was on the horizon.

Investors C. Dean Metropoulos & Co. and Apollo Global Management answered the call—buying select Hostess assets out of bankruptcy and embarking on ambitious plans to return Hostess products to shelves within only a few months.

On July 15, 2013, Hostess treats were once again being sold throughout the country as the iconic brand staged the "Sweetest Comeback in the History of Ever" to the delight of legions of fans. Twinkies had turned back time.

As the fanfare mounted and new boxes flew off of store shelves, it became clear that one sweet comeback deserved another. The idea for *The Twinkies Cookbook, Twinkies 85th Anniversary Edition* was born—a celebration of a sweet sensation, with a country of enthusiasts fueling its astonishing staying power.

We want to thank the thousands of fans who made their voices heard to pave the way for the return of a brand that continues to stand as an icon of Americana. We especially want to thank the culinary wizards who channeled their creativity and opened up their virtual recipe boxes to make the second edition of this cookbook possible.

Here's to the next chapter of Twinkies. Dig in!

Hostess TWINKIES give your customers a real one-two ...and they love it!

Num-ber One! Hostess Twinkies are just great . . . by themselves. As dessert, as a treat in a lunch box, as a between-meal snack . . . your customers love Twinkies . . . and then some!

Num-ber Two! Hostess Twinkies are just great . . . served with fruit . . . with ice cream. Matter of fact, housewives have told us their families eat even more of these favorite desserts when Twinkies are perched on the side of plates!

So . . . it's just good old-fashioned horse sense to get Hostess Twinkies out in plain view . . . on your counter. That's where Twinkies will really go to work for you . . . selling those related items day-in, day-out! Yes, Twinkies have *earned* their reputation as one of the biggest-little-sales-pluggers in the grocery business, today!

Continental Baking Company, Inc.

THEY'RE CREAMED FILLED!

TWINKIES EIGHTY-FIVE YEARS
OF A SWEET SENSATION

What makes Twinkies so special? Everyone has an answer.

If there were a lifetime achievement award for snack cakes, Twinkies would certainly set the gold standard—now more than ever.

Perhaps it's the nostalgia. From comic strips to the silver screen, state fairs to science projects, legal legends to urban legends, artifacts to art exhibits, Howdy Doody to Archie Bunker—Twinkies have been baked into our national pop culture for generations. Who would have thought a simple confection of sponge cake and cream filling could become a national icon?

Of course, one wonders if a few persistent tall tales have had a little something to do with the timeless mystique. For the record, Twinkies don't last forever. Nor are they made with a supersecret chemical compound that makes

them indestructible. Contrary to what Homer may have been told in a memo-rable episode of *The Simpsons*, you can harm a Twinkie.

Maybe it's old-fashioned national pride. As a vintage television spot declared, "Twinkies are American through and through." President Clinton certainly must have thought so when he considered the Twinkie for the National Millennium Time Capsule as an "object of enduring American symbolism."

But why overthink it? After all, we're talking about Twinkies here. Have you tasted one lately? They're incredibly good. If it's been a while, your first bite undoubtedly will be even sweeter than you remembered. Diet mavens may balk, but at 135 calories per Twinkie, you could do a lot worse these days.

Whatever the root of their appeal, Twinkies sparkle with an undeniable magic—a star that seems to shine brighter with age. This is quite astonishing considering the snack cake's inventor was just looking for a way to put idle shortcake pans to use when strawberries were out of season.

● ● ●

The remarkably colorful history of Twinkies dates back to early 1930. Hoovervilles were sprouting from state to state, the Chrysler Building neared completion in New York, and bakery manager James A. Dewar was embarking on the "best darn-tootin' idea" he ever had.

Ten years after starting his career driving a horse-drawn pound cake wagon for the Continental Baking Company outside Chicago, Dewar was at the frontier of almost unimaginable fame. Continental was looking for a new, inexpensive product that would appeal to frugal consumers in the tight economy. Why not use the company's stockpile of shortcake pans to create a treat that could be sold year-round? Dewar thought.

Blending a dry mix of necessity, practicality, and ingenuity, he whipped up the celebrated recipe by injecting smooth and creamy banana filling into the oblong golden finger cakes. Unlike strawberries, which were only in season for six weeks during the summer, bananas were readily available year-round.

As for the name, a St. Louis billboard advertising "Twinkle Toe Shoes" provided all the inspiration Dewar needed. He was quoted as saying he "shortened it to make it a little zippier for the kids."

Dewar's new two-for-a-nickel treat was an instant hit.

"To think [Continental] didn't know if people would like them," recalled Margaret Branco, one of the company's original "Twinkie stuffers," in an interview with the *St. Louis Post-Dispatch*. "We could hardly keep up with the demand. You'd think people had nothing to do but eat Twinkies. They sold like hotcakes."

In the early days, every Twinkie had to be hand-filled using a specially created machine operated with a foot pedal. "You had to pump the pedal just right or too much filling would shoot out," Branco explained. "If I oversquirted, the Twinkie would explode. Of course, that wasn't so bad. I got to eat the crippled ones. I never lost my appetite for them. Not only that, I lost weight. I was a butterball when I started. I got thinner on Twinkies."

As Twinkies marched to snack cake superstardom, Dewar, like a proud parent, remained their number one fan, eating at least three a day for more than fifty years. (He admitted to having "sort of a sweet tooth.")

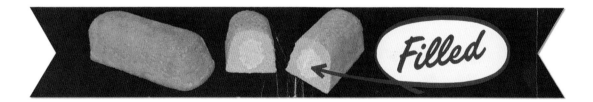

Dewar's grandchildren, in an interview with the *Rochester* (NY) *Democrat & Chronicle*, recalled how "Grandpa Twinkie" never tired of telling the Twinkie story and would regularly visit grocery stores to make sure the little cakes were always fresh. He kept his own stash in the fridge and freezer.

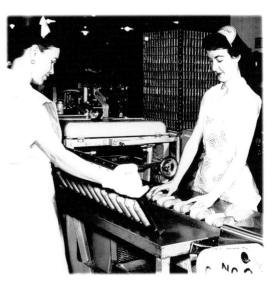

"Some people say Twinkies are the quintessential junk food, but I believe in the things," Dewar once told United Press International. "I fed them to my four kids and they feed them to my fifteen grandchildren. Twinkies never hurt them."

Though Twinkies became one of the most popular products in American history, Dewar reportedly never received any special compensation for his illustrious invention. He retired from Continental in 1972, having become a vice president. But no promotion could ever have topped his title as "Mr. Twinkie."

After Dewar's death in 1985 at age eighty-eight, a Shelbyville, Indiana, man emerged to stake claim to top Twinkie-eating honors. Lewis Browning, a retired milk truck driver who lived well into his nineties, ate at least one Twinkie a day, a custom he began in 1941. That's right, more than twenty thousand Twinkies.

The baton awaits the next would-be Twinkie king, though Browning left considerable shoes to fill.

Not everyone has been so obliging when it comes to Twinkies. Take Twinkiegate: In the 1980s, a grand jury indicted a Minneapolis city council candidate for serving coffee, Kool-Aid, Twinkies, and other sweets to two senior citizen groups. The case led to the passage of the Minnesota Campaign Act, widely known as the Twinkie Law. The seventy-one-year-old candidate, George Belair, lost the election, but the charges against him were eventually dropped.

"How can anyone bribe someone with Twinkies?" he asked in a *Los Angeles Times* article.

Honorable intentions aside, Belair may have seriously underestimated what people would do for a Twinkie—or the raw emotions the little snack cake could evoke.

Just ask *Rocky Mountain News* columnist Mark Wolf. When Hostess experimented with fruit and creme Twinkies several years ago, Wolf fired off an irate headline: "Hey Hostess, here's a tip: Don't mess with my Twinkies."

"To alter a Twinkie is to demean a national resource," the self-described Twinkie-holic wrote. "How could anyone tinker with perfection?"

"Despite occasional attacks by misguided nutritionists and dentists, the original Twinkie reigns as the American snack food and arguably the greatest product of the Industrial Revolution."

To be fair, Hostess thought consumers might appreciate a throwback to the shortcake's roots, but ultimately decided to abandon the idea. No doubt to the comfort of legions of Twinkie purists, the fruit and creme effort was a rare occasion in Twinkie history when the classic cake was, well, "messed with."

With the exception of a change to vanilla filling during World War II, driven by a banana shortage, and the introduction of a "light" variety in 1990, Twinkies have remained remarkably close to the original recipe. And that's just the way people like it—to the tune of five hundred million Twinkies each year.

So let us raise a toast to an American original—the magical, mystifying, magnificent Twinkie.

The journey's been quite a treat.
Let the future be even sweeter.

1

+

cake

● ● ●

Twinkie Carrot Cake Cookies

These cookies are great for everyday snacks or for a kids' event. Twinkies serve as a terrific canvas. Even when you add the cinnamon, carrots, and other ingredients, you can still enjoy the distinctive Twinkie flavor.

—Lisa Hansen, Kansas City, Missouri

10 Twinkies, halved lengthwise

½ cup unsalted butter, softened

¼ cup firmly packed brown sugar

2 eggs, at room temperature

1⅓ cups all-purpose flour

1 teaspoon baking powder

½ teaspoon ground cinnamon

¼ teaspoon ground nutmeg

1 cup shredded carrots
(about 2 medium carrots)

Icing

2 tablespoons cream cheese, softened

1 teaspoon freshly squeezed lemon juice

½ teaspoon pure vanilla extract

1 cup confectioners' sugar

Preheat the oven to 350°F. Line baking sheets with parchment paper.

Use the tip of a table knife to scrape out the cream filling from each Twinkie and place the filling in a bowl. Set aside.

In a food processor, process the butter and brown sugar until mixture is creamy. Add the Twinkie cake pieces and process until the cake is fully incorporated. Add the eggs and process until blended. Scrape down the sides of the work bowl as needed.

In a small bowl, whisk together the flour, baking powder, cinnamon, and nutmeg. Add the flour mixture to the food processor and process just until the dry

continued >>

ingredients are blended into the batter. Add the carrots and pulse just to combine.

Drop the cookies by tablespoonfuls about 2 inches apart on the prepared baking sheets. Flatten slightly using lightly floured fingertips or a lightly floured flat-bottomed glass. Bake for 11 to 12 minutes, until set. Transfer the cookies to a rack to cool completely.

To make the icing, add the cream cheese, lemon juice, and vanilla to the reserved Twinkie filling. Using an electric mixer at medium-high speed, beat until blended and creamy. Beat in the confectioners' sugar, blending well. Spread icing over each cookie.

• Tip •

Store the cookies in an airtight container for up to 3 days.

Twinkie Strawberry Shortcake

When my sister-in-law made this recipe for a family dinner, everyone thought she had worked her tail off in the kitchen. She shared the secret of this quick and easy dessert only with the women. Now it's become our inside joke when we make it—the men think we've slaved away for them.

—Debbie Johnston, St. Augustine, Florida

10 Twinkies, halved lengthwise

1 (16-ounce) package frozen strawberries in syrup, refrigerated until just thawed

1 (8-ounce) container frozen nondairy whipped topping, thawed

Arrange half of the Twinkies, cut side up, in a 9 by 13-inch baking dish. Top with half of the strawberries, then half of the whipped topping. Repeat the layers of Twinkies, strawberries, and whipped topping. Cover and refrigerate until chilled, about 1 hour.

Cut into squares and serve.

• • •

Pineapple Upside-Down Cake Twinkies

Twinkies are shortcakes amped up. Their flavor gets infused into whatever you throw them into—the sugary glaze goes right in the pineapple. This recipe is great for cookouts. Many people wouldn't think to put Twinkies on the grill, but it really works!

–Jen Rattie, Lake Zurich, Illinois

4 tablespoons unsalted butter

¼ cup firmly packed brown sugar

1 (8.5-ounce) can sliced pineapple, drained

4 Twinkies

12 maraschino cherries, drained

Preheat a grill, or allow coals to burn down to low heat.

Cut 4 pieces of aluminum foil, each about 10 by 12 inches. Place 1 tablespoon of butter, cut into quarters, in the center of each piece of foil. Sprinkle 1 tablespoon of brown sugar over the butter, then top with a slice of pineapple. Place a Twinkie, rounded side down, on top of each pineapple slice. Gently press three maraschino cherries into the bottom of each Twinkie, placing them into the spots where the filling was inserted. Wrap the foil up over the Twinkie, folding the top and sides down securely to seal completely.

Place the foil packet on the grill, rounded side of the Twinkie down, and grill 3 minutes. Turn the Twinkie packet over and grill for 2 minutes. Carefully remove from the grill and let stand 1 to 2 minutes. Place each foil packet in a serving dish. Carefully open the foil packet, allowing steam to escape. Serve warm.

• Tip •

Serve topped with a dollop of whipped cream and another maraschino cherry, if desired.

• • •

Ribbons and Bows Twinkie Wedding Cake

This Hostess original recipe is a Twinkie take on a wedding cake. Fondant is a prepared confection, readily available at stores selling cake-decorating supplies, including large craft stores. It comes in a variety of colors and in various package sizes. To use it, place it on a board lightly dusted with cornstarch or confectioners' sugar and roll it to the desired thickness, usually about ⅛ inch thick, with a rolling pin.

7¾ pounds prepared fondant in 2 colors

27 Twinkies

1 (4-inch-diameter, 4-inch-thick) piece Styrofoam

1 (7-inch-diameter) cardboard cake round, covered with decorative, food-safe aluminum foil

1½ (16-ounce) cans buttercream frosting

1 (8-inch-diameter, 4-inch-thick) piece Styrofoam

1 (11-inch-diameter) cardboard cake round, covered with decorative, food-safe aluminum foil

Reserve 1 pound of the fondant and roll the rest out to ⅛ inch thick. Wrap 13 of the Twinkies in strips of one of the colors of fondant (3½ to 4 ounces fondant per Twinkie). Lightly brush the edges of the fondant with water to seal tightly. Wrap the remaining 14 Twinkies in the other color of fondant.

For the top layer, place the 4-inch round of Styrofoam in the center of the 7-inch cardboard round. Frost the top and sides with one-third of a can of frosting. Alternating the colors, arrange 10 of the fondant-wrapped Twinkies upright around the Styrofoam, attaching them with the frosting, with the seams facing in. The top edge of the Twinkies should be even with the top of the frosted Styrofoam.

continued >>

For the bottom layer, place the 8-inch round of Styrofoam in the center of the 11-inch cardboard round. Frost the top and sides with the remaining two-thirds of the first can of frosting. Alternating the colors, arrange the remaining 17 fondant-wrapped Twinkies upright around the Styrofoam, attaching them with the frosting, with the seams facing in. The top edge of the Twinkies should be even with the top of the frosted Styrofoam.

Fill a pastry bag fitted with a #12 tip for larger decorations (or a #4 or #5 tip for more delicate decorations) with frosting. Pipe a decorative filigree of frosting on the top edges of the Twinkies on the bottom layer, or mold fondant into decorative shapes and position on top of the Twinkies.

Stack the top layer on the bottom layer. Fit the pastry bag with a #6 tip. Pipe dots of frosting around the edges of the cardboard circles.

Cut flowers from the fondant with a small cookie cutter and decorate the tops of the Twinkies on the top layer. Fit the pastry bag with a #3 tip and pipe a small dot of frosting in the center of each flower.

To make a bow on top of the cake, roll the reserved 1 pound fondant out to a ⅛-inch thickness and cut into strips about 1 inch wide. Place a generous dollop of frosting on top of the cake, then use a strip of fondant to make a loop, sticking the ends into the frosting to secure. Continue to add loops of fondant ribbon, securing each loop in the frosting, to make a large bow.

● ● ●

Twinkie Tunnel Bundt Cake

I make this cake for special occasions and when company is coming. People love the surprise of finding the Twinkie filling inside the chocolate cake!

–Darlene Casalino, Cape Coral, Florida

1 (18.25-ounce) box chocolate cake mix, batter prepared according to package instructions

6 Twinkies, halved lengthwise

Confectioners' sugar, for dusting

Spray a 12-cup Bundt pan with nonstick vegetable oil spray. Pour half of the cake batter into the prepared pan.

Arrange the Twinkies in a circle in the middle of the batter, cut sides facing out, standing them up vertically so that they are surrounded front and back by the batter. Pour the remainder of the cake batter into the pan. Bake according to the package instructions for cooking with Bundt pans.

Remove from the oven and cool for about 15 minutes in the pan. Invert the pan to remove the cake and transfer to a wire rack to cool completely. Dust the top and sides of the cake with confectioners' sugar and cut into slices to serve.

■   ■   ■

Twinkie Cupcakes

People like the nostalgia of snack cakes in their lunch. This one is for Twinkie lovers—it's a birthday cake with Twinkies in it. They can have Twinkies and cake all in one.

—Owner/baker Heather McDonnell, Cupcrazed Cakery, Fort Mill, South Carolina

1 cup unsalted butter, softened

1½ cups sugar

5 eggs, at room temperature

1½ cups self-rising flour

¼ cup buttermilk

½ cup sour cream

1½ teaspoons pure vanilla extract

1½ cups all-purpose flour

6 Twinkies, quartered

4 cups Marshmallow Buttercream
(page 24)

Preheat oven to 350°F. Line muffin tins with cupcake liners.

In a bowl, using an electric mixer at medium-high speed, beat the butter until fluffy. Add the sugar and beat on medium-high speed for 1 minute. Scrape the sides of the bowl and continue to beat for 2 minutes.

Add the eggs and beat on medium speed until fluffy, about 2 minutes. Add the self-rising flour and buttermilk and mix until combined. Add the sour cream, vanilla, and all-purpose flour. Mix until there are no lumps, scraping sides of bowl occasionally.

Place a small amount (about half to two-thirds of a tablespoon) of batter into each cupcake liner. Place one piece of a Twinkie on top of the batter. Top with a heaping tablespoon of batter, covering the Twinkie piece completely. Bake for 17 to 19 minutes, until top is golden brown and set and a wooden pick inserted into the center comes out clean. Transfer to a cooling rack to cool completely.

Frost or pipe with marshmallow buttercream.

• Tip •

If you do not have self-rising flour on hand, blend together 1½ cups all-purpose flour, 2¼ teaspoons baking powder, and ¾ teaspoon salt. Use this blend in place of the self-rising flour listed in the recipe.

●　　●　　●

Marshmallow Buttercream

1 cup unsalted butter, softened

½ cup marshmallow cream

3 cups confectioners' sugar

Yellow food coloring (optional)

1 tablespoon milk, if needed

In a bowl, using an electric mixer at medium-high speed, beat the butter until fluffy. Add the marshmallow cream and 1½ cups of the confectioners' sugar and beat until smooth. Add the remaining confectioners' sugar and continue to beat until fluffy. If desired, add a few drops of yellow food coloring and beat until blended. Frosting will become smooth and spreadable, but if not, add milk until the desired consistency is reached.

• • •

No-Bake Twinkie Turtle Cake

The Twinkie is great because it pairs with almost any flavor and doesn't need to be baked. This recipe is perfect for a potluck—that way you aren't tempted to eat the whole thing yourself!

—Alesha Jacobsen, Phoenix, Arizona

10 Twinkies, halved lengthwise

1 (5.9-ounce) package instant chocolate pudding mix

3 cups milk

1 (8-ounce) package chopped pecans (about 2 cups)

1 (12.25-ounce) jar caramel ice cream topping, plus more for garnish

1 (8-ounce) container frozen nondairy whipped topping, thawed

½ cup semisweet chocolate chips

Arrange Twinkies, cut side up, in a 9 by 13-inch baking dish.

In a bowl, combine the pudding mix and milk and stir according to the package instructions. Immediately pour the pudding evenly over the Twinkies. Sprinkle the pecans evenly over the pudding. Pour the caramel ice cream topping evenly over the pecans. Spread the whipped topping evenly over the caramel. Sprinkle with the semisweet chocolate chips. Cover and refrigerate for several hours or overnight. If desired, drizzle each piece with more caramel topping.

◦ Tip ◦

Toasting the pecans intensifies their flavor. To toast the pecans, spread in a single layer on a baking sheet. Bake at 350°F for 5 to 7 minutes, until lightly toasted.

• • •

Malted Cake Truffles with Dark Chocolate Hot Fudge

The iconic Twinkie flavor is great on its own, but it can also work as a blank canvas to add other flavors. Malt, fruit, chocolate—the possibilities are endless! I love all things malted, so I liked the idea of adding malt flavor to a Twinkie. I took the existing Twinkie and turned it into two textures, a filling and a crunchy crumble. The Twinkie flavor is still very much recognizable; my truffles are a reimagined version.

— Pastry chef Mathew Rice, Girl & the Goat and Little Goat, Chicago, Illinois

10 Twinkies

2 tablespoons malt powder

2 tablespoons whole milk

2 cups white chocolate, finely chopped

Dark Chocolate Hot Fudge

8 ounces dark chocolate, chopped

½ cup firmly packed light brown sugar

½ cup light corn syrup

½ cup heavy cream

1½ teaspoons cocoa powder

½ teaspoon salt

1 teaspoon vanilla extract

Preheat the oven to 250°F.

Unwrap 5 of the Twinkies and freeze them until they're firm, about 1 hour. Slice thin layers off the tops and sides, being careful not to cut into the cream filling. Reserve the Twinkie middles to make the truffle filling.

Place the sliced cake on a baking sheet in a single layer and toast in the oven until dry and slightly more golden, about 10 minutes. Cool completely and break into crumbs with your hands or by rolling a rolling pin over them. They should be a little coarse and look like bread crumbs.

continued >>

Whisk together the malt powder and milk.

In a bowl, break the Twinkie middles and the remaining 5 Twinkies into small chunks. Pour the milk into the bowl and fold with a spatula until combined. Allow to chill for 10 minutes.

Line a baking sheet with parchment paper. Scoop the chilled mixture into balls, place on the baking sheet, and freeze until firm, about 4 hours. You should have between 10 and 12 truffles, depending on the size.

Melt the white chocolate over a double boiler. Using 2 forks to create a cradle, dip the truffles in the white chocolate, one at a time, and immediately roll them in the Twinkie crumbs. Chill until ready to serve.

To make the fudge, place the chopped chocolate in a small heat-proof bowl. In a small saucepan, combine the brown sugar, corn syrup, heavy cream, cocoa powder, salt, and vanilla. Bring to a simmer. Pour over the chocolate and whisk until smooth.

Truffles are best served cold with hot fudge alongside for dipping.

2

+

pie

● ● ●

Twinkie Cherry Pie

Friends and family love my Twinkie pie. I make it for barbecues, birthdays, and other special occasions.

—Carolyn Nicholson, Inglewood, California

1 (8-ounce) package cream cheese, at room temperature

1 (14-ounce) can sweetened condensed milk

10 Twinkies, halved lengthwise

1 (21-ounce) can cherry or other fruit pie filling

1 (15-ounce) can crushed pineapple in juice, drained

½ cup chopped Brazil nuts or other nuts (optional)

1 (8-ounce) container frozen nondairy whipped topping, thawed

In a bowl, combine the cream cheese and condensed milk and beat with an electric mixer on medium-high speed until smooth. Arrange the Twinkies, cut side up, in a 9 by 13-inch baking dish. Pour the cream cheese mixture over the Twinkies.

Reserve about 1 tablespoon of the pie filling for garnish. Spoon the remaining pie filling over the cream cheese layer. Spoon the pineapple over the pie filling.

Reserve 2 tablespoons of the nuts for garnish. Sprinkle the remaining nuts over the pineapple. Then spread the whipped topping over all. Garnish with the reserved pie filling and nuts.

Cover and refrigerate for 4 to 6 hours or overnight. Cut into squares to serve.

● ● ●

Twinkie Toast Pie

I knew right away that I wanted to make a piecrust out of Twinkies. And I was in a period of my life where I was eating a lot of French toast and was trying to French toast-ify anything I could. I just combined the two. It doesn't taste like anything you've ever eaten before. It tastes like magic. Vive le Hostess!

–John Boone, E! Online, Los Angeles, California

16 Twinkies

½ cup unsalted butter, melted

1 cup heavy whipping cream

2 teaspoons pure vanilla extract

1 tablespoon sugar

3 eggs, at room temperature

½ cup milk

1 teaspoon ground cinnamon

2 tablespoons unsalted butter

Preheat oven to 400°F. Spray a pie pan with nonstick coating.

Cut 10 Twinkies in half lengthwise. Use the tip of a table knife to scoop out the cream filling and place the filling in a small bowl. Set aside.

Break the Twinkie cake halves into small pieces and place in a separate bowl. Use a large spoon to mash the cake into very small, even pieces. Drizzle with the ½ cup melted butter. Continue to stir, mashing to make a mixture that is almost smooth and is the consistency of paste. Spoon the mixture into the prepared pie pan. Using lightly floured fingers, press the cake mixture to form an even crust across the bottom and up the sides of the pan. Bake for 13 to 14 minutes until golden brown and crisp. Set aside to cool completely.

In a deep bowl, using an electric mixer on low speed, beat the cream, 1 teaspoon of the vanilla, and the sugar until frothy. Add the reserved cream filling. Increase to medium-high speed and beat until the mixture forms soft peaks. Cover and refrigerate.

In a bowl, whisk together the eggs, milk, the remaining 1 teaspoon of vanilla, and the cinnamon.

Melt the 2 tablespoons butter in a large skillet over medium heat. Quickly dip the remaining 6 Twinkies, one a time, into the egg mixture, coating completely, then place in the hot skillet. Cook, turning to brown evenly, until edges are crisp but not overbrowned, about 30 seconds on each side. Carefully remove Twinkies to a cutting board and allow to cool slightly. Using a sharp knife, gently cut into bite-size pieces. Place the Twinkie pieces into the reserved cream mixture. Stir until the pieces are almost completely incorporated. Spoon the creamy filling into the baked crust.

Cover with plastic wrap and refrigerate for 2 hours or until well chilled. Cut into wedges.

· · ·

No-Bake Twinkie Pumpkin Pie

This is like a pumpkin pie cheesecake. It has a Twinkie-based bottom and then it's a cream cheese, whipped cream, vanilla combo in the middle with pumpkin pie filling and whipped cream and pumpkin pie spice on the top. This can serve as an easy and tasty potluck item, especially around the holidays!

–Lindsay Bloomfield, E! Online, Los Angeles, California

10 Twinkies, halved lengthwise

1 (8-ounce) package cream cheese, softened

1 cup sugar

1 (8-ounce) container frozen nondairy whipped topping, thawed

2 (3.40-ounce) packages instant vanilla pudding mix

1 (15-ounce) can pumpkin

2 teaspoons pumpkin pie spice, or equal parts ground cinnamon and nutmeg, plus more for garnish

1 cup milk

In a 9 by 13-inch baking dish, place the halved Twinkies, cut side up.

In a bowl, using an electric mixer at medium speed, beat the cream cheese, sugar, and half of the whipped topping until smooth. Spread evenly over the Twinkies.

In a large bowl, combine the pudding mixes, pumpkin, pumpkin pie spice, and milk until smooth. Spoon evenly over the cream cheese layer. Spread with the remaining whipped topping. Sprinkle with additional pumpkin pie spice if desired. Refrigerate for several hours or overnight.

• • •

Twinkie Strawberry Shortcake Pie

This wonderful dessert combines all of the great flavor of strawberry shortcake with a fresh strawberry pie, and the secret ingredient is a layer of Twinkies.

—Roxanne Wyss and Kathy Moore, The Electrified Cooks, Kansas City, Missouri

¾ cup sugar

3 tablespoons cornstarch

5 cups fresh strawberries

½ cup water

2 to 3 drops red food coloring (optional)

4 Twinkies, cut into ½-inch slices

1 (9-inch) single shell piecrust, baked and cooled

1 cup heavy whipping cream

2 tablespoons confectioners' sugar

1 teaspoon pure vanilla extract

In a small saucepan, stir together the sugar and cornstarch.

To make the glaze, chop 1 cup of the strawberries and add to the sugar-cornstarch mixture. Stir in the water. Mash the berries gently using a potato masher or the back of a wooden spoon to release the juice. Cook, stirring constantly, over medium heat, until the mixture bubbles and thickens, 5 to 6 minutes. Stir in the food coloring. Set aside and allow to cool completely.

Arrange the Twinkies, cut sides down, in the bottom of the piecrust. Slice the remaining fresh strawberries and arrange over the Twinkies. Pour the cooled glaze over the strawberries, using a pastry brush or the back of a small spoon to spread the glaze evenly over the top of the pie. Refrigerate 3 hours or until chilled.

In a bowl, using an electric mixer at low speed, beat the cream until it is frothy. Increase speed to medium, gradually add the confectioners' sugar and beat until stiff peaks form. Beat in the vanilla. Pipe or spoon whipped cream over the top of the pie in a decorative fashion.

• Tip •

Prepare your favorite piecrust recipe or a refrigerated, prepared piecrust. Follow the directions to bake a single crust pie shell.

● ● ●

Patriotic Twinkie Pie

While preparing a recipe for a Fourth of July party, I realized I was missing a few key ingredients. It was too late to go to the store, so I began looking for substitutes and used some of the Twinkies I had on hand. Twinkies gave the dessert a distinctive taste, and I've never gone back to the old recipe!

—Ruth Royal, Cody, Wyoming

1 (6-ounce) package blueberry Jell-O

3 cups boiling water

1 (16-ounce) bag frozen blueberries

1 (6-ounce) package strawberry Jell-O

1 (16-ounce) bag frozen sliced strawberries in syrup

6 to 7 Twinkies, broken or torn into 1-inch pieces

2 (5.1-ounce) packages instant vanilla pudding mix

6 cups milk

1 (12-ounce) container frozen nondairy whipped topping, thawed

In a heat-proof bowl, combine the blueberry Jell-O and 1½ cups of the boiling water and stir until dissolved. Add the blueberries and stir until blended and slightly thickened. Allow to cool completely.

In another heat-proof bowl, combine the strawberry Jell-O and the remaining 1½ cups boiling water and stir until dissolved. Add the strawberries and stir until blended and slightly thickened. Allow to cool completely.

Place half of the Twinkie pieces in a 6-quart glass bowl or trifle dish. In a separate bowl, combine the pudding mix and milk and stir according to the

continued >>

<< Patriotic Twinkie Pie, continued

package instructions. Spoon half of the pudding over the Twinkies, spreading evenly. .

Spoon the blueberry mixture over the pudding, spreading evenly. Top with the remaining Twinkie pieces. Spoon the remaining pudding over the Twinkies, spreading evenly. Spoon the strawberry mixture over the pudding, spreading evenly.

Cover and refrigerate for several hours or overnight, until completely chilled and set. Top with the whipped topping just before serving.

3

+

fruit

Twinkie Sushi

I often use Hostess products in my crazy food recipes. They're a great art supply. I love sushi and thought it would be fun to have sushi for dessert. It's nice to serve Twinkie Sushi at a dinner party on a Japanese tray or in a bento box with chopsticks. Guests will laugh while they enjoy a refreshing fruity dessert at the same time.

—Clare Crespo, Baton Rouge, Louisiana

4 pieces green fruit leather, sliced into 1-inch-wide strips

6 Twinkies, cut into 1-inch pieces

Assorted dried fruits, cut into small pieces

Assorted chewy fruity candies

4 to 6 pieces of dried mango, cut into strips, for garnish

One at a time, wrap the fruit leather pieces around the Twinkie pieces. Place the wrapped Twinkies upright on a serving tray or in a bento box.

Place the dried fruits and candies into the cream filling. Garnish the tray with strips of dried mango to resemble pickled ginger. Serve with chopsticks if you wish.

• • •

Twinkie Easter Egg Hunt

I've always been a loyal Twinkie fan. I originally came up with this recipe as a way to get our children seated and quieted down after they finished their Easter egg hunt. It's become a family tradition. By changing the food coloring and decorations, you can use it to make something special for any holiday.

–Maxine Frank, Clearwater, Florida

10 Twinkies

Spray food coloring in a variety of colors

3 (7-ounce) jars marshmallow cream

20 maraschino cherries, well drained

6 ounces semisweet chocolate chips

½ cup jelly beans

1 (5.9-ounce) package instant chocolate pudding mix

3 cups milk

Spray the Twinkies with the food coloring, using a variety of colors. Cut each Twinkie in half crosswise.

Spoon the marshmallow crème into a 9 by 13-inch baking dish, covering the bottom completely. Arrange the Twinkies, cut side down, in the crème, leaving the tops sticking up so they look like Easter eggs. Decorate around the Twinkies with the maraschino cherries, chocolate chips, and jelly beans.

In a bowl, combine the pudding mix and milk. Stir according to the package instructions. Chill the mixture until thickened.

To serve, spoon 3 tablespoons of the pudding into each bowl. Scoop up a Twinkie along with some of the marshmallow cream and candies and add to each bowl.

SERVES
20

Apple Brie Cheddar Minis

The first time I tried a Twinkie, I was about four years old—and I was obsessed. Who would have thought grilled cheese would work so well on a Twinkie? The apple, brie, and cheddar give it a bit of sophistication—and the nuts give it an added texture.

—Lorraine Caton, Brooklyn, New York

10 Twinkies, halved lengthwise

1 large unpeeled Granny Smith apple, quartered and cored

3 tablespoons unsalted butter

3 tablespoons dark rum

⅔ cup shredded sharp cheddar cheese

4 ounces brie cheese, cut into 10 thin slices

¼ cup chopped walnuts, toasted

2 tablespoons balsamic vinegar

1 tablespoon honey

1 teaspoon fresh minced rosemary

1 teaspoon Sriracha hot sauce

Salt

Use the tip of a table knife to scoop out the cream filling from each Twinkie and place the filling in a small bowl. Set aside.

Place the 10 Twinkie bottom portions on the work surface and set the rounded tops of each Twinkie aside.

Cut each apple quarter into 5 thin slices. Melt 1 tablespoon of the butter in a skillet over medium heat. Add apple slices and cook 4 to 5 minutes, until apples are just tender, turning slices to cook evenly. Stir in rum. Cook for 1 minute. Remove from the heat and set aside.

Sprinkle about 1 tablespoon of cheddar cheese on the bottom portion of each Twinkie. Top the cheese with 2 slices of apple. (If there is any collected liquid, drizzle a little over each Twinkie.) Place one slice of brie on top of the apples. Sprinkle each with about 1 teaspoon of walnuts, dividing equally among the Twinkies. Place the top on each Twinkie, making a sandwich.

Melt the remaining 2 tablespoons of butter in a large skillet over medium heat. Place the Twinkie "sandwiches" in the skillet. Cook until golden brown and the cheese is melted, 2 to 3 minutes, turning to brown evenly. (Work in batches, if necessary, and add butter, if needed.) Remove from the skillet and keep warm.

Meanwhile, in a small saucepan, stir together the vinegar and honey. Heat over medium-low heat, until mixture just begins to simmer. Cook, stirring frequently, for 3 minutes or until mixture is reduced slightly and is the consistency of syrup. (Watch carefully so it does not boil dry.)

Stir together the reserved cream filling with the rosemary, and add the Sriracha and salt to taste.

To serve, cut the Twinkie sandwiches into quarters, securing each with a long toothpick. Arrange on serving plates and drizzle with the balsamic honey syrup.

continued >>

Pipe or dollop the cream filling mixture on each Twinkie sandwich. Serve immediately.

● Tips ●

To easily pipe the filling, spoon filling into a sandwich bag. Seal and clip the corner. Gently squeeze the filling onto each Twinkie sandwich.

If desired, substitute 1½ tablespoons balsamic vinegar reduction for the balsamic vinegar and honey in this recipe. There's no need to simmer it or reduce it further, just drizzle over the Twinkie sandwiches.

You can purchase balsamic vinegar reduction at the grocery store, or you can make your own by bringing 1 cup balsamic vinegar and 2 tablespoons brown sugar or honey to a low boil. Reduce heat and allow to simmer 20 to 30 minutes, until the mixture is reduced by half. Allow to cool. Cover and store in the refrigerator. This is also excellent as a glaze on grilled salmon or meats, or use it in salad dressings.

Twinkie Orange Bavarian Dream

I've made this dessert using various flavors of Jell-O, but this particular version was inspired by my stepmother, who loves the combination of orange and vanilla and often reminisces about eating Dreamsicles as a girl.

–Anna Ginsberg, Austin, Texas

10 Twinkies, halved lengthwise

1 (15-ounce) can mandarin oranges, drained

1 (3-ounce) package orange Jell-O

½ cup boiling water

1 (3.4-ounce) package instant French vanilla pudding mix

1½ cups milk

½ cup French vanilla liquid coffee creamer

1 (12-ounce) container frozen nondairy whipped topping, thawed

Place the Twinkies cut side up in a 9 by 13-inch baking dish. Layer half of the oranges over the Twinkies.

In a heat-proof bowl, combine the Jell-O and boiling water and stir to dissolve. Cover and refrigerate for 10 minutes to cool.

In a large bowl, beat together the pudding mix, milk, and coffee creamer for 2 minutes, until slightly thickened. Add the Jell-O to the pudding mixture. Stir until smooth. Fold in two-thirds of the whipped topping until combined. Spread the mixture over the Twinkies and oranges. Cover and refrigerate for 6 to 8 hours, until set.

Just before serving, spread the remaining whipped topping over the top. Decorate with the remaining oranges and cut into squares to serve.

●　●　●

County Fair Parfait

I was raised in the South and grew up with Hostess, so I thought about fusing memories with a dish. Going to the county fair is a fun, quintessential childhood moment that I wanted to share here—and even pass on to my nine-year-old daughter.

—Shelly Flash, Brooklyn, New York

5 Twinkies

1 cup frozen nondairy whipped topping, thawed

1 pint blueberries

1 quart strawberries, sliced

Preheat oven to 375°F. Line a baking sheet with parchment paper.

Place one Twinkie on the prepared baking sheet. Bake, uncovered, for 6 to 8 minutes, until the Twinkie is toasted and the outside is crisp. Set aside and allow to cool completely.

Cut the remaining 4 Twinkies into ½-inch pieces. In each of 4 (16-ounce) wide-mouth canning jars, layer in order, 2 to 3 tablespoons Twinkie pieces, 1 heaping tablespoon whipped topping, ¼ cup blueberries and ½ cup strawberries. Repeat each layer. Top each with a dollop of whipped topping.

Using a fine Microplane grater, grate the edges of the crisp, baked Twinkie to make crumbs. Garnish the top of each layered dessert with the crumbs.

If desired, cover each jar for easy transport to a picnic, potluck, or other event.

Garnish the top of each dessert with a mint leaf.

• • •

Twinkie Kebabals

This was a spur-of-the-moment idea. I had leftover fruit, but not enough Twinkies to give each of the gals at my candle-making party her own. This recipe saved the day.

–Dianne Meyers, Lakemoor, Illinois

10 Twinkies

20 large marshmallows

About 60 pieces or chunks of fruit, such as strawberries, pineapple, kiwi, and pitted cherries

Cut each Twinkie crosswise into quarters. Thread alternating pieces of Twinkies, marshmallows, and fruit onto wooden skewers. Serve immediately.

• • •

Banana Twinkie Bread Pudding

This recipe can also be flambéed: Place the rum and liqueur in a long, heat-proof ladle and carefully light it with a long match. Pour the flaming spirits into the banana mixture and shake the skillet gently until the flame subsides.

—Diane Halferty, Corpus Christi, Texas

10 Twinkies, cut into bite-size pieces

3 cups milk

3 eggs

⅔ cup sugar

2 very ripe large bananas

1 tablespoon ground cinnamon

¼ teaspoon ground nutmeg

½ teaspoon pure vanilla extract

½ cup dried cherries or sweetened dried cranberries

½ cup pecans, lightly toasted

3 tablespoons unsalted butter, cut into small pieces

Preheat the oven to 300°F. Butter a 9 by 13-inch baking dish. Place the Twinkie pieces in a large bowl.

To make the Twinkie pudding, in a blender, combine the milk, eggs, sugar, bananas, cinnamon, nutmeg, and vanilla and process until smooth. Pour over the Twinkie pieces. Fold in the cherries and pecans. Transfer the mixture to the prepared baking dish and let stand for 20 minutes. Top with the butter.

Cover the baking dish with aluminum foil and place it into a larger pan. Put the pans in the oven and pour hot water into the larger pan to a depth of 1 inch. Bake for 1 hour, then remove the foil and bake uncovered for 15 to 20 minutes, until a knife inserted just off center comes out clean.

Topping

¾ cup heavy whipping cream

1 tablespoon sugar

¼ teaspoon pure vanilla extract

Sauce

⅔ cup unsalted butter, at room temperature

½ cup firmly packed light brown sugar

6 ripe large bananas, sliced

1 teaspoon ground cinnamon

¼ teaspoon ground nutmeg

3 tablespoons dark rum, or 1 tablespoon rum extract

2 tablespoons banana liqueur or strawberry-banana juice

1 teaspoon pure vanilla extract

To make the topping, whisk or beat the cream in a bowl just until it begins to thicken. Add the sugar and vanilla and continue beating until soft peaks form. Cover and refrigerate.

To make the sauce, heat a large sauté pan or skillet over low heat. Add the butter and brown sugar and cook, stirring gently, until melted and smooth. Add the bananas, cinnamon, and nutmeg and cook for 1 to 2 minutes, until the bananas just begin to soften. Stir very gently so as not to break up the bananas. Remove the pan from the heat and add the rum and liqueur. Return the pan to the heat, add the vanilla, and stir well. Remove from the heat and keep warm.

To serve, place a large scoop of the Twinkie pudding in the middle of each plate or bowl. Spoon some sauce over each piece. Top with the whipped cream and serve immediately.

4

+

chocolate

• • •

Chocolate Twinkie Pudding

I was six months pregnant when I came up with this idea and was craving anything choco-laty, gooey, and warm. Just throw everything into a slow cooker, turn it on, and in no time you'll have a fabulous dessert.

—Amy Ott, Greenfield, Indiana

8 Twinkies

3 eggs, at room temperature

2 cups milk

1½ teaspoons pure vanilla extract

½ cup sugar

½ cup packed brown sugar

3 tablespoons unsweetened cocoa

½ cup semisweet chocolate chips

Spray a 4-quart slow cooker with nonstick vegetable spray. Cut the Twinkies into bite-size pieces and place in the slow cooker.

In a bowl, whisk the eggs. Stir in the milk, vanilla, the sugars, and the cocoa. Pour the milk mixture over the Twinkies. Sprinkle with the chocolate chips.

Cover and cook on high for 2½ to 3 hours. Unplug the slow cooker and allow to stand, covered, for 30 minutes. Serve warm.

● ● ●

Twinkie Burritos

I have always loved Twinkies with chocolate and strawberries. One day while at my wife's Mexican restaurant, I tried wrapping the mixture in a tortilla so I could eat it with my hands. Even though my wife laughs at me, Twinkie burritos are delicious, and now all of her employees and I are hooked!

—Peter Sheridan, Washington, DC

---

4 (10- to 12-inch) flour tortillas, warmed

½ to ¾ cup chocolate sauce

4 Twinkies

2 cups sliced strawberries, or ½ cup strawberry preserves

Drizzle one side of each tortilla with the chocolate sauce. Place a Twinkie on top of the chocolate sauce in the center of each tortilla. Top each Twinkie with ¼ cup of the strawberries. Fold the tortillas over the Twinkies and roll up like a burrito.

• • •

Fried Twinkies with Chocolate Sauce

I came up with this dessert one night after discovering I was out of the ice cream balls I use to make fried ice cream, one of my favorite desserts. I grabbed some Twinkies I had in the cabinet as a substitute and, wow, were they great! Now, whenever I have a cookout or a group of friends over, I serve chocolate fried Twinkies.

—Karl E. Moser, Conway, South Carolina

About 4 cups vegetable oil, for deep frying

4 Twinkies

¼ cup confectioners' sugar

Chocolate syrup

Whipped cream, for garnish (optional)

Pour the oil into a deep fryer or saucepan. It should be deep enough to half-cover a Twinkie. Heat on high or over high heat until the oil reaches 375°F.

Carefully place 1 or 2 of the Twinkies in the hot oil without crowding them. Fry for about 20 seconds on each side, turning to brown evenly. Remove and drain on paper towels. Repeat with the remaining Twinkies. Allow the Twinkies to cool briefly.

Place each Twinkie on a small dessert plate and dust with the confectioners' sugar. Drizzle with the chocolate syrup, garnish with the whipped cream, and serve immediately.

• • •

Twinkie Brownie Bars

Growing up in Canada, we would cross the border to buy Twinkies as a special treat. These are great for potluck, kids' birthday parties, and family events. My family ate them straight out of the pan.

—Tamara Litke, Lewisville, Texas

1 (18.3-ounce) box fudge brownie mix, batter prepared according to package directions

1 (11-ounce) package caramels, unwrapped (about 38)

1 tablespoon milk

9 Twinkies, halved lengthwise

1 (1.25-ounce) envelope powdered hot chocolate

1 (8-ounce) container frozen nondairy whipped topping, thawed

Spray the bottom only of a 9 by 13-inch baking dish with nonstick spray. Pour in the brownie batter and bake according to package directions. Allow brownies to cool 15 to 20 minutes.

Place the caramels and milk in a microwave-safe glass bowl and microwave on high power (100%) for 1 to 1½ minutes, stirring every 30 seconds until melted and smooth. Spread evenly over the brownies.

Arrange the Twinkies, cut side down, in the caramel, making 2 rows of 9 each.

Stir the hot chocolate mix into the whipped topping. Spread evenly over the Twinkies. Cover with plastic wrap and refrigerate several hours or overnight.

Twinkie Petits Fours

I created this recipe in honor of my dad, using his favorite treats—Twinkies and chocolate. They are so good, and no one believes me when I tell them what they are.

—Barbara Canfield, Bakersfield, California

2 Twinkies

4 ounces milk or dark chocolate (or 1 cup chips), chopped

Whipped cream

4 maraschino cherries, halved

Freeze the Twinkies for 1 hour, until firm. Line a baking sheet with waxed paper.

Slice each Twinkie crosswise into ¾-inch pieces. Place the chocolate in a small, microwave-safe bowl and microwave on high power (100%) for 30 seconds. (If you're using both milk and dark chocolates, melt them in separate bowls.) Stir, then continue to microwave for 15 seconds at a time, stirring frequently, until smooth.

Dip each piece of Twinkie into the melted chocolate, then place on the prepared baking sheet. Decorate the tops of some of the petits fours with swirls or drizzles of the chocolate. Place in the freezer for at least 5 minutes, until firm.

Top the undecorated petits fours with a dollop of whipped cream and a cherry half. Serve immediately.

Chocolate Hazelnut Twinkie S'mores

After school, my grandmother would take me to the neighborhood bodega to get a Twinkie every day. We would do creative things with a Twinkie like make a layered cake, cake pops, or stack them like Jenga. I cried when Twinkies were off the shelves. When they returned to stores, I thought to myself, Thank God, the world is right again . . . Twinkies are back. It didn't seem right not to be able to share something I loved when I was a kid with my own kids.

—Vanessa Diaz, Sherman Oaks, California

4 double squares graham crackers

3 tablespoons chocolate hazelnut spread

1 Twinkie, quartered

4 marshmallows

Split each graham cracker in half. Spread a heaping teaspoon of chocolate hazelnut spread on one side of each cracker half. Place a Twinkie slice on 4 graham cracker halves.

Place 1 marshmallow on each of the remaining 4 halves. Place a marshmallow-topped cracker on a small, microwave-safe glass plate. Microwave on high power (100%) for 8 to 10 seconds or until marshmallow is just hot and melted.

Place marshmallow half on top of a Twinkie-topped cracker and press lightly. Repeat with the remaining ingredients.

Twinkie-Choconana Toffee Crunch

I got married and the big joke is that I only know how to make reservations. So this recipe was a surprising breakthrough. Chocolate and banana is my favorite combination, and I thought it would be awesome to add a Twinkie to my favorite blend of flavors. If I do say so myself, it's delicious!

–Michele Isbrecht Greenbaum, East Norriton, Pennsylvania

10 Twinkies, halved lengthwise

1 (22-ounce) container prepared chocolate pudding

4 bananas, sliced

1 (6.5-ounce) can whipped cream

⅔ cup milk chocolate English toffee bits

Arrange half of the Twinkies, cut side up, in a 9 by 13-inch baking dish.

Spread one-third of the pudding over the Twinkies, covering completely. Arrange half of the banana slices in a single layer over the pudding. Repeat the layering with the remaining Twinkie halves, another one-third of the pudding, and the remaining banana slices. Spread the remaining pudding over the top of the bananas.

Decorate with the whipped cream and sprinkle the toffee bits over the top. Serve immediately.

5

cream

SERVES
4

Twinkie Banana Split

My grandma, Memo, and I invented and perfected this recipe a long time ago. Memo is now gone, but the recipe lives on. I work for my dad, who is a farmer and rancher, and this is an easy dessert to prepare at the end of a long day feeding livestock and cultivating thousands of acres of farmland. You can add a "grown-up" touch by adding rum to the whipped topping.

–Karen Oney, Fort Worth, Texas

4 Twinkies

4 bananas, halved lengthwise

1 quart vanilla ice cream

1 (12-ounce) jar strawberry ice cream topping

1 (12-ounce) jar pineapple ice cream topping

1 cup frozen nondairy whipped topping, thawed

½ cup chopped cashews

4 maraschino cherries

Place 1 Twinkie in each of 4 banana split dishes and arrange a banana half on either side of each Twinkie. Place 2 small scoops of ice cream on top of each Twinkie. Top with the strawberry and pineapple toppings and a dollop of whipped topping. Sprinkle on the cashews and top with a cherry. Serve immediately.

● ● ●

Twinkie Bomb

I came up with this recipe for my goddaughter's third birthday. It was a great activity for the kids to take part in—messy and fun.

—Zephir Plume, Boulder, Colorado

6 Twinkies, well chilled

½ cup raspberry jam

2 cups vanilla ice cream, slightly softened

Fresh raspberries, for garnish (optional)

Vanilla cream sauce or raspberry dessert sauce, for garnish (optional)

Line 4 parfait dishes with plastic wrap. Cut each Twinkie crosswise into 10 pieces. Arrange a layer of Twinkie pieces in each parfait glass, covering the bottom and sides. Spread the raspberry jam over the Twinkies, filling in any crevices. Spoon the ice cream into the center of each Twinkie-covered parfait. Arrange the remaining Twinkie pieces to completely cover the parfaits. Freeze for about 20 minutes, until firm.

Remove from the freezer and place upside down on dessert plates. Remove the dishes and peel the plastic wrap off each dessert. Garnish with raspberries and vanilla cream sauce and serve immediately.

● ● ●

Twinkie Forest Berry Ice Cream

I used to eat Twinkies all the time as a kid. When I was young, my Grandpa and I used to sneak Twinkies into the movie theaters. Now, I do it with my son.

–Jenne Kopalek, Lewisville, Texas

1 cup blueberries

1 cup raspberries

1 cup blackberries

1½ tablespoons sugar

2 cups heavy whipping cream

1 (14-ounce) can sweetened condensed milk

3 Twinkies, cut into ½-inch slices

Preheat the oven to 350°F. Line a 9 by 13-inch pan with aluminum foil and spray with nonstick spray. Line a 10 by 5-inch loaf pan or a 9 by 9 by 2-inch baking dish with plastic wrap or parchment paper, extending the plastic or paper up the sides.

Place all of the berries in the 9 by 13-inch pan. Sprinkle evenly with the sugar. Bake, uncovered, for 8 minutes. Remove from the oven. Carefully, using the back of a fork, mash the berries evenly. Set aside.

In a bowl, using an electric mixer at low speed, beat the cream until it is frothy. Increase speed to medium and beat until thickened and soft peaks form.

continued >>

<< Twinkie Forest Berry Ice Cream, continued

Pour about one-third of the milk into the beaten cream and stir gently with a spoon until blended. Add the remaining milk and very gently, using a spoon, fold into the cream. Set aside.

Spoon about one-third of the cream mixture into the prepared loaf pan. Arrange slices from 1 Twinkie across the cream. Top with about one-third of the berries and juice. Repeat the layers two more times, ending with the berries. Cover the top gently with plastic wrap.

Freeze for 4 to 24 hours, until the ice cream becomes firm throughout.

To serve, lift using the edges of the plastic wrap or parchment paper and invert onto a serving platter. Allow to stand 5 minutes to soften slightly. Slice into pieces. Serve immediately.

Twinkiehenge

Some believe Twinkiehenge was created as an archaic sundial, designed to provide my ancestors with the precise time to serve and eat dessert. But this theory is widely refuted, as even casual observers can see that any time is considered the right time for dessert in the Brakeville clan. Twinkiehenge is a great dessert for relatives and supreme alien beings alike.

–Barry Brakeville, Lenexa, Kansas

1 (5.9-ounce) package instant chocolate pudding mix

3 cups milk

12 to 16 chocolate sandwich cookies, crushed into fine crumbs

3 to 4 Twinkies, halved crosswise

In a bowl, combine the pudding mix and milk and stir according to the package instructions, until thickened. Pour the pudding into a 1½-quart serving bowl.

Sprinkle the crushed cookies over the pudding, covering the surface completely. Plunge the Twinkie pieces, cut side down, into the pudding, arranging them in a circle with the rounded edges protruding from the pudding.

● ● ●

Twinkie Lasagna

When I was a child, my mother always packed Twinkies in my lunch. As I matured, I wanted to incorporate my fondness for Twinkies into an adult treat. People love it when I make this dessert; it brings back sweet memories.

—Diana Pillittieri, Jamestown, New York

10 Twinkies, halved lengthwise

1 (12-ounce) bag semisweet or milk chocolate chips

1 cup sliced fresh strawberries

1 cup fresh raspberries

1 (3.4-ounce) package instant vanilla pudding mix

2 cups milk

1 (8-ounce) container frozen nondairy whipped topping, thawed

Arrange the Twinkies, cut side up, in a 9 by 13-inch baking dish.

Place the chocolate chips in a microwave-safe bowl and microwave on high power (100%) for 1 minute. Continue to microwave for 15 to 30 seconds more, stirring frequently, until melted and smooth. Drizzle the chocolate over the Twinkies, then layer the strawberries and raspberries over the chocolate.

In a bowl, combine the pudding mix and milk and stir according to the package instructions, until thickened. Pour the pudding over the berries, then spoon the whipped topping over the pudding. Refrigerate for 2 to 3 hours, until set.

Twinkie Bread Pudding with Whiskey Sauce

In high school, I always had a Twinkie as a pregame snack before sports events. The boost worked for me. I made this one year for Thanksgiving and it was gone within five minutes.

—Adam Everett, Frisco, Texas

1 cup plus 2 tablespoons sugar

1½ teaspoons ground cinnamon

3 eggs, at room temperature

1 egg yolk, at room temperature

2½ cups milk

2½ cups heavy whipping cream

1 tablespoon pure vanilla extract

12 Twinkies, quartered

¼ cup dark raisins

¼ cup golden raisins

½ cup chopped, toasted pecans (optional)

2 tablespoons butter, melted

Preheat the oven to 350°F. Spray a 9 x 13-inch baking dish with nonstick spray.

In a small bowl, stir together the 2 tablespoons sugar and ½ teaspoon of the cinnamon; set aside.

To make the bread pudding, in a large mixing bowl, whisk together the eggs, egg yolk, and the remaining 1 cup of sugar, whisking until well blended. Whisk in the milk, cream, vanilla, and the remaining 1 teaspoon of cinnamon.

Stir the Twinkie pieces, raisins, and pecans into the egg-milk mixture. Allow to stand 15 minutes.

Pour the Twinkie mixture into the prepared baking dish. Drizzle with the melted butter. Sprinkle with the

½ cup butter

2 tablespoons water

1 egg, at room temperature

¾ cup sugar

2 tablespoons bourbon or whiskey
(or 1 teaspoon brandy extract)

reserved cinnamon-sugar mixture. Bake, uncovered, for 55 to 60 minutes, until set and lightly brown. Remove from oven and allow to stand 30 minutes.

Meanwhile, make the sauce. Melt the butter in a small saucepan over low heat. Remove from the heat and allow to cool for about 10 minutes.

In a small bowl, whisk together the water and egg. Whisk the egg mixture and sugar into the melted butter. Cook over medium-low heat, stirring constantly, until mixture comes to a boil, 6 to 7 minutes. Remove from heat and stir in the bourbon. Allow to cool for 10 minutes.

To serve, spoon warm bread pudding into dessert dishes and top with the sauce.

● Tip ●

Toasting the pecans intensifies their flavor. To toast the pecans, spread in a single layer on a baking sheet. Bake at 350°F for 5 to 7 minutes, or until lightly toasted.

● ● ●

Twinkie-Misu

When my sister returned from living in Italy for a time, she grew homesick for the desserts she had enjoyed there. So I decided to try my hand at tiramisu, but replaced the lady-fingers with Twinkies, which we had all grown up on. She liked it just as much as the original!

—Zephir Plume, Boulder, Colorado

1 (3.4-ounce) package instant vanilla pudding mix

1¾ cups milk

¼ cup almond-flavored liqueur

1 cup strong coffee, warmed

1 tablespoon sugar

¼ cup Kahlúa

2 cups frozen nondairy whipped topping, thawed

10 Twinkies

Unsweetened cocoa, for dusting

In a bowl, whisk together the pudding mix, milk, and liqueur. Set aside until quite thick.

In a separate, small bowl, combine the coffee, sugar, and Kahlúa and mix until the sugar dissolves. Refrigerate until cool. Line a baking sheet with waxed paper and set the Twinkies on the paper. Slowly drizzle the coffee mixture over each Twinkie, allowing the liquid to soak in.

Fold the whipped topping into the pudding mixture. Spoon one-third of the pudding mixture into an 8 by 8-inch baking dish. Arrange the Twinkies evenly over the pudding. Spoon the remaining pudding mixture over the Twinkies.

Refrigerate for 1 hour, until set. Dust with cocoa just before serving.

• • •

Bite-Sized Twinkie Baked Alaska

We have had large family get-togethers at our lake cottage for years and fried Twinkies are a menu favorite. This recipe takes the Twinkie up a notch and could provide a new tradition for years to come.

–Deb Thompson, Cadillac, Michigan

2 Twinkies

1 cup ice cream (select your favorite flavor)

2 egg whites, at room temperature

2 tablespoons sugar

Pinch of cream of tartar

Line a baking sheet with parchment paper.

Cut a thin slice off the round ends of each Twinkie. Cut each Twinkie into 4 even slices. Place slices several inches apart on the prepared baking sheet. Scoop about 2 tablespoons of ice cream on top of each slice and mound to resemble a round scoop. (Using a cookie scoop makes this step easy). Cover with plastic wrap and freeze several hours or overnight.

When ready to serve, preheat the oven to 500°F. In a bowl, using an electric mixer at high speed, beat egg whites until frothy. Continue beating and gradually add sugar and cream of tartar. Beat until stiff peaks form.

Cover each Twinkie bite with the meringue. Bake for 2 minutes, until the meringue browns. Serve immediately.

● ● ●

Frozen Yogurt Twinkie Pop

This creamy frozen treat is a popular classic—made even better with Twinkies. It is the perfect combination of healthy fruits and yogurt combined with the goodness of Twinkies!

—Roxanne Wyss and Kathy Moore, The Electrified Cooks, Kansas City, Missouri

---

1 cup frozen unsweetened strawberries, partially thawed, reserving juices

1 banana

1 tablespoon honey

2 (5.3-ounce) cartons vanilla nonfat yogurt

2 Twinkies, cut into ½-inch slices

6 ice pop molds or 5-ounce paper cups

6 food-safe craft sticks

Place the strawberries, with collected juices, and banana in a food processor and process until the strawberries are evenly chopped. Add the honey and yogurt and process until blended.

Add the Twinkie pieces and pulse just until Twinkies are moistened and evenly blended into the yogurt mixture.

Spoon the Twinkie-yogurt mixture into the ice pop molds. Insert a stick into each pop. Freeze several hours or overnight.

Remove from the molds (or cut away paper cups). Serve immediately.

● ● ●

Twinkie Ice Cream

Two of my favorite desserts have always been Twinkies and ice cream, so I decided to combine them to create Twinkie ice cream. It tastes wonderful and has been a huge hit at my store, Country Cow Creamery, where we make all of our ice cream, pies, cakes, and other baked goods from scratch.

—Edward Dubrowski, Colonia, New Jersey

2 tablespoons all-purpose flour

2 tablespoons cold water

2 cups milk

¾ cup sugar

2 egg yolks, lightly beaten

1 cup heavy whipping cream

1 teaspoon pure vanilla extract

4 Twinkies, broken into 1-inch pieces

In a small bowl, combine the flour and cold water and stir until a smooth paste forms. Prepare a double boiler over simmering water.

Pour the milk into a saucepan and heat over low heat until warm. Add the flour paste and blend well. Cook, stirring constantly, for about 15 minutes, until the milk is hot and slightly thickened. Transfer the mixture to the top of the double boiler and cook, stirring frequently, for 15 minutes, until bubbles start to form around the edges. Don't let it come to a full boil. Stir in the sugar.

Blend a small amount of the hot milk mixture into the beaten egg yolks. Then blend all of the egg yolk

continued >>

mixture back into the hot milk mixture. Cook, stirring constantly, for 2 minutes. Pass the custard through a fine-mesh sieve into a bowl. Cover and refrigerate for 1 to 2 hours, until well chilled.

Stir the cream and vanilla into the custard mixture. Transfer to a 2-quart ice cream maker and freeze according to the manufacturer's instructions. When the ice cream is almost frozen, stir in the Twinkie pieces. Freeze until firm.

6

+

meat

Chicken-Raspberry Twinkie Salad

I often try to create new recipes from odds and ends that I have in the refrigerator, and that's how this dish came about. I am a former Peace Corps volunteer who has served in several Latin American countries, so making do with things and survival-style preparation come naturally to me. I was out of Wonder Bread one day and improvised using Twinkies. It turned out great.

–Gary Gonya, Baltimore, Maryland

½ cup raspberry preserves

¼ cup balsamic vinegar

6 Twinkies, halved lengthwise

2 cups shredded cooked chicken

2 Roma tomatoes, seeded and diced

1 jalapeño pepper, seeded and diced

2 tablespoons chopped red onion

Salt and freshly ground black pepper

1 cup shredded cheddar cheese

2 cups mixed baby greens

Preheat the oven to 450°F.

In a small bowl, whisk together ¼ cup of the raspberry preserves and 2 tablespoons of the vinegar to make a raspberry vinaigrette. Set aside.

With a small spoon, scrape the filling out of the Twinkies and reserve in a bowl. Place the Twinkies, cut side up, on a baking sheet.

Add the remaining ¼ cup of raspberry preserves and 2 tablespoons vinegar to the reserved cream filling. Mix until well blended, then add the chicken and mix well.

continued >>

In a separate bowl, combine the tomatoes, jalapeño, and onion and mix well. Season to taste with salt and pepper.

Place a spoonful of the chicken mixture in each Twinkie half. Sprinkle the cheese over the Twinkies, dividing evenly. Spoon the tomato mixture over the top, dividing evenly.

Place in the oven and bake for about 5 minutes, until the cheese melts.

Arrange a bed of the mixed greens on 6 plates. Remove the Twinkies from the oven and place 2 halves on each bed of greens. Drizzle with the raspberry vinaigrette and serve immediately.

● ● ●

Chicken & Winkies

Twinkies are a great additive when you don't want to use plain sugar to sweeten something like a milk shake, an ice cream sundae, or Chicken & Winkies. This is just an everyday meal for those who like breakfast for dinner or vice versa.

—Andres DeLeon, The Original Baby's Cheesesteak & Lemonade, Orland Park, Illinois

2 eggs, at room temperature

2 cups all-purpose flour

1 tablespoon sugar

4 teaspoons baking powder

¼ teaspoon salt

2 Twinkies, crumbled

1¾ cups milk

½ cup unsalted butter, melted

10 hot, fully-cooked chicken tenders

Maple syrup or pancake syrup

Separate the eggs into yolks and whites; set aside.

In a bowl, whisk together the flour, sugar, baking powder, salt, and crumbled Twinkies. Add the egg yolks, milk, and butter; blend well.

In another bowl, using an electric mixer at high speed, beat the egg whites until stiff peaks form. Fold the egg whites into the batter.

Preheat a waffle iron according to the manufacturer's directions. Add the suggested amount of batter and bake until browned and crisp. Remove baked waffles and keep warm.

Top each waffle with chicken tenders and serve with maple syrup.

• • •

Twinkie Corndog

I wanted to do a savory application, something fun to highlight the taste and texture of a Twinkie. The batter is made with whole Twinkies. The beauty of this recipe is that you can use any sausage that you like and dip it in the batter—hot dogs, veggie dogs, chicken sausage, even a cheddar brat.

–Chef Miguel Trinidad, Maharlika Filipino Moderno and Jeepney Filipino Gastropub, New York, New York

6 Twinkies, quartered

¾ cup milk

2 large eggs, at room temperature

¾ cup cornmeal

1 teaspoon salt

1 teaspoon baking powder

8 to 10 (6- to 8-inch) skewers

8 to 10 hot dogs or bun-length fully cooked smoked sausages

Vegetable oil for deep frying

1 cup all-purpose flour

Honey Mustard Dipping Sauce (recipe follows)

Combine the Twinkies, milk, eggs, cornmeal, salt, and baking powder in a blender. Blend until mixture is smooth. Pour batter into a deep bowl.

Insert a skewer lengthwise into each hot dog, leaving a 2- to 3-inch handle.

Heat the oil in a deep fryer according to the manufacturer's directions or in a large saucepan, over medium heat, until the oil reaches 300°F to 325°F.

Place the flour in a shallow plate or pie pan. Roll each hot dog in the flour, coating evenly. Dip the flour-covered hot dog into the batter, coating evenly and allowing excess to drip back into the batter.

continued >>

<< Twinkie Corndog, continued

Carefully place the batter-dipped hot dog in the hot oil. Fry until golden brown, 4 to 5 minutes, turning to brown evenly. Remove from oil and place on a paper towel–lined plate. Repeat with the remaining hot dogs. Allow to cool slightly before serving. Serve with the dipping sauce.

To make the sauce, stir together all of the ingredients.

Honey Mustard Dipping Sauce

2 tablespoons whole grain mustard

1 tablespoon honey

1 tablespoon calamansi* or freshly squeezed lime juice

*Calamansi is a specialty citrus fruit that is popular in Filipino and Malaysian dishes.

● ● ●

Pigs in a Twinkie

My twelve-year-old nephew Shea created this recipe because he thought it would be something other kids would enjoy. It's important to cook the sausage thoroughly.

–Janine O'Barr, Burbank, California

6 pork sausage links

6 Twinkies

Maple syrup, for serving

Preheat the oven to 350°F.

Place the sausage in a skillet over medium heat and cook, turning to brown evenly, until the meat is no longer pink inside, following any package directions. Remove from the skillet and drain well on paper towels.

Thinly slice one end off of each Twinkie. Stuff a cooked sausage into each Twinkie. Place the Twinkies in a shallow baking dish and bake for 10 minutes, until the Twinkies are warm. Serve warm, with syrup.

Deep-Fried Bacon-Wrapped Chocolate-Covered Twinkies

I wanted to take Twinkies to a level no man has ever gone before. It seems beyond possibility, but it's still a Twinkie. People say, "You can't go wrong with bacon," but you also can't go wrong with Twinkies and chocolate. This combines the best of both worlds.

–Chef George Duran, New York, New York

Vegetable oil for deep frying

4 Twinkies, frozen

2 slices bacon, halved

1 (12-ounce) package semisweet chocolate chips

Heat the oil in a deep fryer according to the manufacturer's directions or in a large saucepan, over medium heat, until the oil reaches 375°F.

Wrap each frozen Twinkie with half a slice of bacon. Use skewers or long toothpicks, as needed, to secure the bacon.

Carefully deep-fry a bacon-wrapped Twinkie until the bacon is fully cooked, 1 to 2 minutes, turning to cook evenly. Remove from the oil and set on the paper towel–lined plate to cool. Repeat with the remaining Twinkies. Allow to cool slightly.

Pour the chocolate chips into a deep microwave-safe glass bowl. Microwave on high power (100%) in 30-second intervals, stirring after each, until the chocolate is melted.

Frost each bacon-wrapped Twinkie with the melted chocolate. Serve Immediately.

• Tip •

If desired, garnish with stripes of melted white chocolate and finely chopped crisp, cooked bacon or bacon bits.

Crazy Twinkie Caprese Bites

At our café, which caters to the Eastern Michigan University crowd, we're always trying to come up with new and innovative dishes. Bacon, balsamic vinegar, and basil are all ingredients that go well with sweets, so we thought it would complement the Twinkie. Growing up in the United States, almost all kids had a Twinkie in their lunch box, so we wanted to come up with a dish that taps into that nostalgia.

–Chef Dylan Thompson and Owner Danielle Teachout, Café Ollie, Ypsilanti, Michigan

1 tablespoon unsalted butter

2 Twinkies, cut into ½-inch slices

1 Roma tomato, halved lengthwise and sliced into semicircles

6 slices bacon, cooked crisp and crumbled

4 fresh basil leaves, finely minced

1½ tablespoons balsamic vinegar reduction (see Tip on page 99)

In a nonstick skillet, melt the butter over medium-high heat. Add the Twinkie slices to the skillet and cook until golden brown on both sides. Transfer to a serving plate.

Place a tomato semicircle on top of each Twinkie slice. Top each tomato slice with the crumbled bacon and sprinkle with basil. Drizzle the balsamic vinegar reduction over all. Serve immediately as a delicious appetizer.

You can purchase balsamic vinegar reduction at the grocery store, or you can make your own by bringing 1 cup balsamic vinegar and 2 tablespoons brown sugar or honey to a low boil. Reduce heat and allow to simmer 20 to 30 minutes, until the mixture is reduced by half. Allow to cool. Cover and store in the refrigerator. This is also excellent as a glaze on grilled salmon or meats, or use it in salad dressings.

• • •

Dave's Twinkie Burger

During a sales meeting at the food service company I work for, we had to split up to make a burger using the different ingredients we had on hand. My team won by using Twinkies as the bun to give it a totally different taste than just a precooked burger.

–Dave Edwards, Portland, Oregon

1 frozen, fully cooked beef patty

3 Twinkies, sliced lengthwise

3 slices bacon, cooked until crisp

1½ ounces brie cheese, thinly sliced

2 tablespoons mayonnaise

½ teaspoon green pepper hot sauce, such as Cholulu

½ teaspoon Sriracha sauce

Heat the beef patty, according to package directions, until hot. Set aside and allow to stand 1 minute. Slice the patty into ½-inch strips.

Arrange the strips of the hot beef patty on the bottom half of each Twinkie. Top with a strip of bacon and a slice of brie.

In a small bowl, stir together the mayonnaise, green pepper hot sauce, and Sriracha. Spread the sauce over the cut side of the top half of each Twinkie, then place, cut side down, over the brie.

● ● ●

Twinkling Turkey

I have always loved to cook and experiment often. I came up with this new twist on an old favorite for my boyfriend, who loves Twinkies. Although I have no children, my nieces spend weekends with me and we often cook together. I want them to learn how to cook with different ingredients than what is considered standard. Adding Twinkies to an entrée is one of those unusual combinations that worked out very well indeed!

—Carol Macomber, Belvidere, Illinois

1 (8.5-ounce) package yellow corn muffin mix, prepared and baked according to package instructions

6 Twinkies, halved lengthwise

1 (14- to 18-pound) turkey

1 tart apple, peeled, cored, and diced

¼ cup honey

Remove the muffins from the oven and allow to cool on a wire rack.

Preheat the oven to 350°F. Scrape the cream filling out of the Twinkies with a small spoon and reserve in a small bowl.

Cut the Twinkie cake halves into cubes and spread in a single layer on a baking sheet. Bake for 8 to 10 minutes, until lightly toasted. Remove from the oven and allow to cool completely. Decrease the oven temperature to 325°F.

Rinse the turkey. Crumble the muffins into a bowl, add the apple and toasted Twinkie cubes and mix lightly. Loosely stuff the mixture into the turkey and truss the legs. Place the turkey, breast side up, on a rack set in a roasting pan. Roast the turkey for 12 to 15 minutes per pound, until the thigh temperature reaches 175°F to 180°F and the juices run clear.

In a small bowl, combine the honey with the reserved cream filling and mix well. Brush the turkey with the honey mixture during the last 10 to 15 minutes of roasting time.

Remove the turkey from the oven and let stand for 20 minutes before carving.

7

+

novelty

• • •

Creamy Malted Twinkies Milk Shake

Twinkies were always one of my favorites growing up. I was always really excited to find one in my school lunch box. My kids loved the idea of having this as an after-school snack or treat to celebrate a small victory, like a good grade on a test.

—Tara Kuczykowski, Canal Winchester, Ohio

1 cup vanilla ice cream

½ cup milk

2 tablespoons malted milk powder

1 Twinkie

Whipped cream, for garnish

Candy sprinkles, for garnish

In a blender, combine the ice cream, milk, malted milk powder, and Twinkie and process until smooth. Pour into a tall glass and top with the whipped cream and sprinkles. Serve immediately.

Twinkie Pancakes

This recipe was inspired by Shrek Twinkies, which were made with green filling and in stores when the movie came out on DVD. One night I had a movie party for my grandkids. The next morning I wanted to make something memorable for breakfast, so I created Twinkie pancakes. The kids said the green color spots made them look really cool.

—Jerry Ferrill, Columbus, Ohio

6 Twinkies

4 cups prepared pancake batter

Butter or margarine, for serving (optional)

Pancake syrup, for serving (optional)

Slice each Twinkie crosswise into 8 thin slices. Spray a griddle or skillet with nonstick vegetable oil spray or brush lightly with vegetable oil. Heat the griddle over medium-high heat.

Pour ¼-cup measures of the pancake batter onto the hot griddle, spacing them apart. Arrange 3 Twinkie slices in each pancake. Cook until the pancake begins to bubble and is golden brown on the underside. Carefully turn the pancakes and cook the second side. Serve immediately with butter and syrup.

• • •

Twinkie Grasshopper

My family loves chocolate and mint together. When we make shakes, we like to thicken them up with cakes and cookies. Twinkies just seemed to be the perfect complement to our grasshopper concoction.

—Lori Kimble, Mascoutah, Illinois

2⅓ cups milk

6 Twinkies

4 chocolate-covered mint cookies

2 tablespoons chocolate syrup

3 cups vanilla ice cream

In a blender, combine 2 cups of the milk and the Twinkies and blend for 5 to 10 seconds. Add the cookies and syrup and blend until smooth; then add the ice cream and blend until smooth once again. Pour in the remaining ⅓ cup of milk and blend until thoroughly mixed. Serve immediately.

Twinkirito

I love Twinkies and loved the idea of serving them warm because you don't often see that. Kids go crazy for this.

—Amy Erickson, Albuquerque, New Mexico

---

4 Twinkies

4 egg roll wrappers

Vegetable oil for deep frying

Confectioners' sugar or a cinnamon-sugar mixture, for dusting (optional)

Place a Twinkie diagonally on the egg roll wrapper toward one point. Wrap the Twinkie, pulling up the sides and making a tight packet as you go. Seal the edges with water.

Heat the oil in a deep fryer according to the manufacturer's directions or heat the oil in a large saucepan, over medium heat, until the oil reaches 350°F.

Add one or two of the egg roll wraps to the hot oil and fry until golden brown. Use a slotted spoon and carefully remove the wraps. Place them on a plate lined with paper towels, and allow to cool slightly.

Just before serving, dust with confectioners' sugar. Serve warm.

• • •

French Twinkies

This tasty snack is surprisingly easy to make and sure to bring a smile to even the grumpiest little ones in the morning. I like to prepare it on special occasions, such as birthday breakfasts.

—Janine O'Barr, Burbank, California

---

2 tablespoons unsalted butter

4 Twinkies

2 eggs, lightly beaten

Pancake syrup or confectioners' sugar, for serving

Melt the butter in a skillet over medium heat. Dip each Twinkie into the eggs, coating evenly. Immediately place the Twinkies in the hot skillet and cook until lightly browned and crispy on each side, turning to cook evenly. Serve warm, drizzled with syrup or dusted with confectioners' sugar.